This book belongs to:

Name

Age

Congregation

Exercise Patience!

Regional Convention

Location

Dates

David Waited On Jehovah

1 Samuel 24:2-15, 25:1-35, 26:2-12, Psalm 37:1-7

Notes:

Who were Abraham and Sarah and how did they show patience?

_____

_____

_____

_____

Write or draw something you learned about Abraham and Sarah:

Abraham and Sarah

Who was Joseph and how did he show patience?

_____

_____

_____

_____

Write or draw something you learned about Joseph:

Joseph

Who was Job and how did he show patience?

_____

_____

_____

_____

Write or draw something you learned about Job:

Job

Who was Paul and how did he show patience?

_____

_____

_____

_____

Write or draw something you learned about Paul:

Paul

Who were Mordecai and Esther and how did
they show patience?

_____

_____

_____

_____

Write or draw something you learned
about Mordecai and Esther:

Mordecai and Esther

Who were Zechariah and Elizabeth and how did they show patience?

_____

_____

_____

_____

Write or draw something you learned about Zechariah and Elizabeth:

Zechariah and Elizabeth

Who was Jacob and how did he show patience?

_____

_____

_____

Who was Esau and how did he show impatience?

_____

_____

_____

Write or draw something you learned
about Jacob and Esau:

Be Like Jacob, Not Esau!

Who was Moses and how did he show patience?

_____

_____

_____

Who was Korah and how did he show impatience?

_____

_____

_____

Write or draw something you learned
about Moses and Korah:

Be Like Moses,
Not Korah!

Who was Abel and how did he show patience?

_____

_____

_____

Who was Adam and how did he show impatience?

_____

_____

_____

Write or draw something you learned
about Abel and Adam:

Be Like Abel, Not Adam!

Who was Samuel and how did he show patience?

_____

_____

_____

Who was Saul and how did he show impatience?

_____

_____

_____

Write or draw something you learned
about Samuel and Saul:

Be Like Samuel, Not Saul!

Who was Jonathan and how did he show
patience?

_____

_____

_____

Who was Absalom and how did he show impatience?

_____

_____

_____

Write or draw something you learned
about Jonathan and Absalom:

Be Like Jonathan, Not Absalom!

Who was Micah and how did he show patience?

_____

_____

_____

_____

Write or draw something you learned about Micah:

Micah

Who was Hosea and how did he show patience?

_____

_____

_____

_____

Write or draw something you learned about Hosea:

Hosea

Who was Isaiah and how did he show patience?

_____

_____

_____

_____

Write or draw something you learned about Isaiah:

Isaiah

Who was Ezekiel and how did he show patience?

_____

_____

_____

_____

Write or draw something you learned
about Ezekiel:

Ezekiel

Who was Jeremiah and how did he show patience?

_____

_____

_____

_____

Write or draw something you learned about Jeremiah:

Jeremiah

Who was Daniel and how did he show patience?

_____

_____

_____

_____

Write or draw something you learned
about Daniel:

Daniel

Be a good listener!

Color in a square every time you hear the name:

Jehovah

Jesus

Be a good listener!

Color in a square every time you hear the word:

Patience

Bible or Scripture

"Commit Your Way To Jehovah"

Draw or write about your favorite characters, scenes
and lessons from the drama.

Videos

Draw or write about some of your favorite characters, scenes and lessons from the videos.

Videos

Draw or write about some of your favorite characters, scenes and lessons from the videos.

Videos

Draw or write about some of your favorite characters, scenes and lessons from the videos.

Videos

Draw or write about some of your favorite characters, scenes and lessons from the videos.

Videos

Draw or write about some of your favorite characters, scenes and lessons from the videos.

Friends

Draw or write about some of the old friends you saw
or new friends you made at this convention.

Exercise Patience

WORD SEARCH

Find and circle the words.

M	T	F	J	M	I	G	S	S	T	U	D	Y
O	F	R	I	E	N	D	S	T	H	E	R	R
T	I	T	I	K	H	L	A	B	S	H	R	A
H	S	H	W	G	N	O	D	T	E	A	C	H
L	K	C	F	S	W	E	V	T	S	P	I	D
R	E	A	D	U	P	L	U	A	I	P	C	E
P	G	E	E	E	H	O	G	R	H	Y	O	N
S	O	R	K	R	B	V	H	J	T	R	U	D
M	Y	P	A	T	I	E	N	C	E	E	S	U
A	U	N	T	S	B	E	E	E	R	O	I	R
K	U	N	C	L	L	A	R	K	Y	A	N	E
G	C	O	N	V	E	N	T	I	O	N	T	H

- patience
- love
- Bible
- Jehovah
- preach
- teach
- read
- endure
- friends
- study
- happy
- convention

Notes

Notes

Notes

Notes

Notes

Notes

Notes

Notes

Notes

Notes

Notes

Answers To Word Search

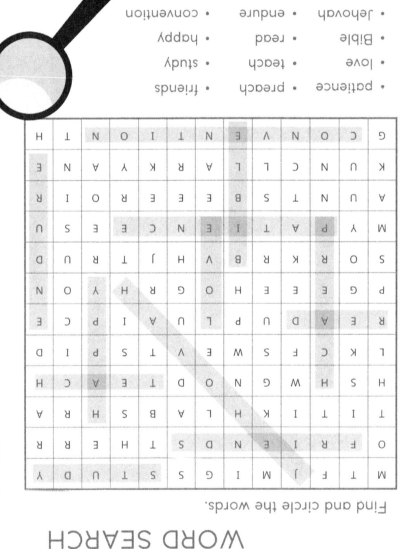

- Jehovah
- Bible
- love
- patience
- endure
- read
- teach
- preach
- convention
- happy
- study
- friends

Find and circle the words.

Exercise Patience
WORD SEARCH

Printed in Great Britain
by Amazon

26551415R00040